Primary Kid's Box 2

Teacher's Resource Pack

Kathryn Escribano with Caroline Nixon & Michael Tomlinson

CAMBRIDGE
UNIVERSITY PRESS

CAMBRIDGE UNIVERSITY PRESS
Cambridge, New York, Melbourne, Madrid, Cape Town, Singapore, São Paulo, Delhi

Cambridge University Press
The Edinburgh Building, Cambridge CB2 8RU, UK

www.cambridge.org
Information on this title: www.cambridge.org/9780521749756

First published 2009

Printed in Poland by Drukarnia GARBINO

A catalogue record for this publication is available from the British Library

ISBN 978-0-521-74975-6   Teacher's Resource Pack 2
ISBN 978-0-521-74947-3   Pupil's Book 2
ISBN 978-0-521-74958-9   Activity Book 2
ISBN 978-0-521-74968-8   Teacher's Book 2
ISBN 978-0-521-74982-4   Audio CDs 2
ISBN 978-0-521-74986-2   Flashcards 2
ISBN 978-0-521-74965-7   Language Portfolio 2
ISBN 978-0-521-68836-9   Interactive DVD 2

Thanks and Acknowledgements

The authors would like to express their warmest thanks to Susan González, Liane Grainger
and Meredith Levy for their encouragement, efficiency and editing skills. They would
also like to thank Melanie Sharp for the beautiful artwork and design.

Kathryn Escribano wishes to thank the staff and children at the CP Narciso Alonso Cortés, Valladolid
(Spain) on whom the ideas have been tried and tested. Finally, she would like to acknowledge the
patience and understanding of her family and friends from whom time was taken to write this book.

The authors and publishers are grateful to the following illustrators:

Melanie Sharp, c/o Sylvie Poggio; Gary Swift; Lisa Williams, c/o Sylvie Poggio; Emily Skinner,
c/o Graham-Cameron Illustration; Lisa Smith, c/o Sylvie Poggio; Chris Garbutt, c/o Arena.

The publishers are grateful to the following contributors:

Pentacor**big**: concept design, cover design, book design and page make-up
Melanie Sharp: cover illustration
John Green and Tim Woolf, TEFL Tapes: audio recordings
Robert Lee: song writing

Contents

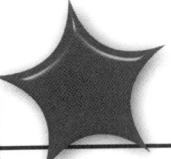

Introduction

This Teacher's Resource Pack is designed to help you and your pupils make the most of *Primary Kid's Box 2*. There are two main sections in this Pack:
  - Worksheets
  - Word cards

Worksheets

- There are two reinforcement worksheets and two extension worksheets per unit. The former are designed to help those pupils who need extra practice whilst the latter are designed to cater for the needs of fast finishers. However, these worksheets not only provide a resource for mixed-ability classes but also offer material to set as homework or for the rest of the class to use while you work individually with a pupil on a speaking test.

- Reinforcement worksheets 1 and 2 for each unit focus on key vocabulary, as does Extension worksheet 1. Extension worksheet 2 offers further exploitation of the unit story.

- There is also a song worksheet for each unit. These always give the song lyrics and a song-based activity which varies from unit to unit. These worksheets are best done once pupils are familiar with the song. The songs are provided on the CD with the Teacher's Resource Pack but you can also use the Class CD.

- There is a page of teaching notes before the worksheets for each unit. These notes include optional follow-up activities which encourage interaction between pupils and add a useful dimension to the worksheet. You may find that one type of follow-up activity works better than another with your particular class, in which case you can use the suggestions as a springboard for adapting other worksheets.

- You may find, according to the particular interests of a pupil, that in one unit, he/she needs a reinforcement worksheet whilst in other units the same pupil can more profitably do an extension worksheet. Fast finishers may want/need to do reinforcement and extension worksheets.

- You can also use the worksheets as gap-fillers or as alternative activities when, for example, some other activity has interfered with the normal running of the class.

- They can be used as models for you or your pupils to develop more worksheets. Creating exercises is an excellent way for pupils to consolidate their learning and they will enjoy swapping them with their friends.

- You may find it useful to keep a record of the unit worksheets each pupil has completed.

- After the resources for each unit, there are two worksheets for each of the following festivals:
  - Halloween
  - Christmas
  - Easter

- The teaching notes for this section contain cultural notes on the festivals which you can use to introduce the topics to the class.

Word cards

- For each unit, there are photocopiable word cards with the key vocabulary items of each unit. These are to support you in the introduction of literacy in English in the classroom. The set includes the vocabulary of the early units for those teaching situations where literacy in English begins at the start of the year, but you may prefer to wait until later units with your class. You may wish to mount the photocopied words on card and laminate them so that they can be used over and over again. You may also like to enlarge them on a photocopier before doing so.

- Some ideas for using the word cards:
  - Display them in the classroom and then, when checking answers, you can ask pupils to point to the corresponding word card or to select it from cards laid out on the table.
  - Do 'word trails' by asking pupils to point to a series of words in succession as you name them.
  - Ask pupils to match word cards with picture flashcards.
  - Reveal one letter at a time, asking pupils to spell out the word or guess it.
  - If you can use a larger space, you could put the word cards around the walls of a gymnasium or a hall and ask pupils to run, hop, jump, etc. from one to another.
  - Alternatively, they can follow a trail of letters to reach the complete word card at the end.

- It is easy to put away one set of word cards as you move on to a new unit, but remember that it is very useful to mix them in with subsequent vocabulary sets. You can then use them to recycle and test vocabulary throughout the year.

 # Teacher's notes

Reinforcement worksheet 1

- Pupils look at the chart and cross out the letters which appear more than once. They write the remaining letters on the dashes and then unjumble them to discover the hidden colour.

Key: brown, black.

- *Optional follow-up activity:* Pupils prepare a similar puzzle. First they write the colour they have chosen, then they fill in the remaining squares. Pupils swap and complete the puzzles.

Reinforcement worksheet 2

- Pupils read the colours at the top of the page and follow the spaghetti lines to the pencils underneath. They colour each pencil accordingly and write the name of the colour on the dashes.

Key: 1 blue, 2 brown, 3 white, 4 green, 5 grey, 6 yellow, 7 pink, 8 orange, 9 purple, 10 red, 11 black.

- *Optional follow-up activity:* Pupils work in pairs, A and B. Pupil A spells one of the colour words. Pupil B identifies the correct colour and finds an example of it in the classroom. Pupils A and B exchange roles.

Extension worksheet 1

- Pupils write the three numbers at the top of the page, putting one letter on each dash. They then use those same letters to fill in the gaps in the second part of the exercise. Finally, they write the words in the correct column in the table.

Key: Colours: red, purple, yellow, blue, grey, pink, green, orange, white, brown,
Numbers: fifteen, eleven, thirteen, seventeen, ten, nineteen, sixteen, fourteen, eighteen, twelve, twenty.

- *Optional follow-up activity:* Pupil A chooses a colour, writes it on a slip of paper and counts how many items there are of that colour in the classroom. He/she then says the number aloud and Pupil B has to guess the colour. Pupils then swap roles.

Extension worksheet 2

- This can be done as a listening exercise (track 1) or a reading exercise. Pupils read each of the speech bubbles and decide which scene it belongs to. They write the scene number in the small accompanying box.

Key: 2, 5, 6, 3, 1, 4.

- *Optional follow-up activity:* Pupils work in groups. They take it in turns to read one of the speech bubbles. The first person to say the next line of the dialogue in the story has the next go.

Song worksheet

- Explain that the letter *b* rhymes with another seven letters (the letters are best friends) while the letter *f* rhymes with another six letters.

- Pupils listen to the chant (track 2) and circle the letters which rhyme with *b*. The second time, they circle the letters which rhyme with *f*. Ask pupils to write the rhyming letters on the dashes and to colour the letters which rhyme with *b* one colour and those which rhyme with *f* another.

Key: Letters rhyming with *b*: c, d, e, g, p, t, v. Letters rhyming with *f*: l, m, n, s, x, z.

- *Optional follow-up activity:* Pupils work in groups. They create a chant for *b*'s or *f*'s best friends. Pupils perform their chants to the class.

Reinforcement worksheet 1

 Find and write.

Example

a	k	n	c	m	h	e	i	g
r	f	j	p	e	q	k	d	l
g	l	d	f	b	a	q	j	s
h	o	c	s	i	w	p	m	e

The letters are <u>r</u> <u>o</u> <u>n</u> <u>b</u> <u>w</u> . The hidden colour is <u>b</u> <u>r</u> <u>o</u> <u>w</u> <u>n</u> .

Now it's your turn.

d	l	h	f	g	e	m	p	o
r	s	n	o	k	q	i	s	t
a	g	e	h	m	j	d	n	b
q	j	c	i	p	f	t	r	g

The letters are _ _ _ _ _ . The hidden colour is _ _ _ _ _ .

Now choose another colour and prepare a puzzle for your friend.

Choose from: grey   red   white   blue   pink   orange

 Match, colour and write.

grey   green   red   white   yellow   blue

brown   black   pink   orange   purple

1 _ _ _ _ _   **2** _ _ _ _ _ _   **3** _ _ _ _ _ _   **4** _ _ _ _ _

5 g r e y   **6** _ _ _ _ _ _ _   **7** _ _ _ _ _ _   **8** _ _ _ _ _ _

9 _ _ _ _ _ _   **10** _ _ _ _   **11** _ _ _ _ _ _